MAKING MONEY ONLINE REVEALED

BY JUSTIN AUTREY

FOREWORD BY KRISTOFER ERICKSON

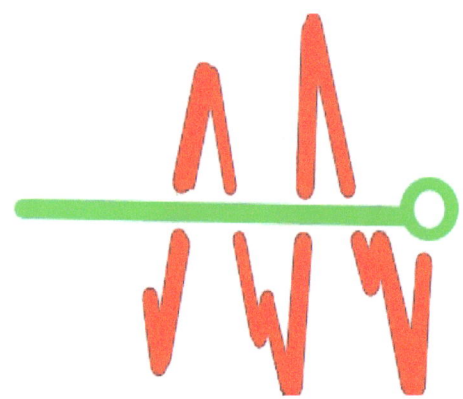

AMERICAN ARTISTS INCORPORATED

Infamous-Ink.com is a division of American Artists Incorporated. All rights reserved. No part of this book may be reproduced or transmitted in any form or by any electronic, or mechanical means, including photocopying, recording or by any information storage and retrieval system, without written permission from the publisher. Copyright laws prohibit any reproduction of this book.

Edited by Kathy Hammond

MAKING MONEY ONLINE REVEALED

BY Justin_Autrey

contact@infamous-ink.com
info@infamous-ink.com

email: contact@infamous-ink.com
Phone: (509) 560-5155

Foreward by Kristofer A. Erickson

CONTENTS
- Solid Foundations
- The Hype
- Smoke & Mirrors
- Harsh Reality
- Basics & Necessities
- Websites
- Options

Appendix
References

FOREWARD

Hi, my name is Kris Erickson. I am 28. I am currently piecing my life back together after some "not so well thought out choices".

I would like to take this time to tell you a little of my story and to enlighten you on a topic that is entirely too close to home for most of us.

Of things we all overlook that could ultimately help bring stability to our lives. Now, I'm not talking about giving up your money or your first born.

I'm talking about simple things each and everyone of us can do with "little or no money". To help bring a more stable lifestyle to each of you, and how Justin Autrey's book "An Ex-Con's Guide to Financial Stability" not only changed my life, but how it changed my way of thinking.

"FROM THE CAGE TO THE STAGE" opened my eyes. It's crazy how we let people control how we make money, and what we do with it.

It's not your fault, trust me. I was coached by Justin in person. He showed me how those very few elite individuals got to the thrones they sit upon.

He also showed me how to take my life back into my own hands and begin the climb up the very same ladder these elite few used to achieve their empires.

His book gave me a much-needed Reality Check for this is what I failed to consider. It's a harsh realization, but you all need to be aware of the same nightmare I was awakened to.

"We"...you, me, them...all of us have dropped the ball. No, I'm not being metaphorical. This is not cryptic writing this is dead set reality. We gave up.

We gave up caring what our future could be, and that's just the tippy top of the iceberg because in the grand tapestry of life. It's not even our future, it's our children's and their children's.

When did what "I" can get here and now become so important? This is the example we are setting to our children. How does that sit in your stomach? For me, it's like a red-hot cannonball.

I don't know about you, you may not have children, but I do, and believe me, I do not want my child's future to depend on the words "would you like fries with that"... or "would you like to supersize your order"

Don't get me wrong, I enjoy the convenience of fast food, especially on long days, but it's no vision in which I would place my loved ones' future. The Next Generation
 are the ones we say we are working for, or at least that's what we tell ourselves. "A Glorious Lie."

If we took just a couple of risks every day to step out of our comfort zones, we too could be as well off as the people we all slave for.

Here are some of the things Justin, whom now is a very good friend of mine, taught me.

Between the covers of this book are the keys to bring light back into your lives, and steps we all can take to become financially stable for our children.

He taught me how to think for myself and how to think for my future. Now when I am released, I will step out of these gates for the first time as a man. A man with a chance and a new direction.

Even better, I did it with minimal effort and almost nothing to call my own. Because of him, I am an author. My first book, Justin and I wrote together, for my children.

A book called "Sam and Bandit Save The Day". A book that can be passed down through generation after generation. My children can read it to their children.

Justin gave me a voice, something we all long for. His books teach a wealth of information from Business to Consulting, investing, even publishing.

If it's management you wish to learn, his books will benefit you. If it's working hands on, or hands off, yes, I said hands off, Justin Autrey can teach you how to succeed on a job site or from your bathtub. It is up to you to choose.

Our futures belong to us. It's up to us to take them back.

Kristopher Erickson
November 3, 2019

SOLID FOUNDATIONS

To date, it is still true that less than 10% of the world's populace control 90% of the money.

That is a sad truth you, and all, will need to come to understand. Do not fret. Whether you know this, or not, it will only affect the choices you make from this point.

At least, it should. Let's face it, you have been living in this world this way for quite some time. You must remember, you choose how to proceed from here.

Yes, you will still have to pay taxes, mortgage, rent, (etc). The bills will never go away. However, the manner in which you pay them, can. IF every pay day, you get your check and drive to the bank in a zombielike state, dreading what pitiful amount of money will be left for you after Uncle Sam takes his cut, and your bills are paid. You are not alone. However, you can be done with feeling that way.

In this book are several factors of modern economy, several myths and realities we all should embrace with a positive attitude. A positive attitude will produce a positive solution.

Yes, "we" are being screwed out of our hard-earned money, but we can change that with a little effort and some guidance. The length of time it takes to turn around this stagnant quagmire of despair relies solely on you.

Today, right here, right now, I will teach you how to do what "they" do. Now, it took me a long time to understand what was really going on behind the big curtain of those "Rich & Famous" individuals who claim to have it all figured out. I will show you in this book. First, you need a SOLID FOUNDATION.

For me, my foundation started with a dream. My parents were poor, and they had a shackle around their ankles. Both tried to drown out their struggles with substances.

I would never blame my circumstance on them. I'm a grown man, and I thank them for their love. However, their extracurricular activities left us with even less to pay bills, or even feed ourselves.

A dream starts here. For me, it is to provide for my family, my children's children, and their loved ones. My dream is to give them the option to choose what they want to do. So that they can live life "shackled" to happiness. Yes, I said happiness.

It's time to take back our own realities. Whether for you or your children to come. It's up to us to leave something behind.

So, what'll it be folks? Gain a voice, because no matter our differences, we are all individuals with our own hopes and dreams.

If you've got it all figured out, this book is not for you. BUT, if you've got it all figured out, stop paying your property tax and see for yourself the harsh reality.

Now, by no means am I telling you to not pay your taxes. That is highly illegal. I am only stating the truth. If you believe you own something, deny the State Government their cut. I bet your beliefs will change very quickly.

Can I show you how to not pay taxes? No, that is entirely not complicated to do. In fact, it's down-right simple. Again, I am in no way, shape, or form telling you not to pay taxes.

Can I show you how to pay less taxes? Sure, it is possible to pay less taxes. This theory depends on several different circumstances.

Can I show you how to make enough money that you won't even bat an eye paying taxes? Absolutely. Now the question to ask yourself is "What do I want to do?" I know people, I'm taking you back to grade school, only I'm asking you to choose what you "really" want to do! Not what you can stomach putting up with, but what you love to do. For it is this, that will bring joy into your life.

Everyone I know wants to make lots of money. All for different reasons. Each, very important to whom it belongs. I think I can speak for 90% of our world's population when I say, "I want to be millionaire so #@!?-/ bad." Though I'm sure for very different reasons. Now the truth is, you need to build a foundation that will last, or survive the fallout!

A steady job is a definite track to surviving the fallout. But what if I told you, you could maximize your achievements with minimal effort, and minimal capitol to reach your goals.

Once you decide what you want to be when you grow up, you can take a leap into the unknown or stay right where you are, shivering in fear over the balance in your bank account.

There are risks involved when you step out of your comfort zones. It is scary not knowing what could happen. But what is worse, taking a chance at being able to afford sending your children to the college they want, or forcing them to suffer wearing secondhand clothes to school year after year?

What I will show you in this book can change your entire outlook on life. It did mine.

Remember what I said, "a job is a bonus"? Yeah, I said bonus because I made my dreams come true with almost nothing. A Solid Foundation should be the first thing you work on. Trust me when I say, even if it is McDonalds. I like McDonalds, who doesn't. And thank you to those people who slave over our burgers and fries, in my opinion, for way too little in return.

If you are like me though, I want to call the shots. I'm a Boss. Yes, I'm a Boss. From nothing but an ex-con to owning 3 businesses in a little over a year. Was it hard? Yes! Though not for reasons I'm sure are rattling around in your head.

I was a cigarette smoker and I lived pack to pack literally. All I wanted was a way up. So, I started looking into making money online. God, to talk about this now is so comical because I remember the frustration I felt when I was "trying to get somewhere". I can remember screaming into the phone at complete strangers trying to explain that I speak English poorly. Yes, I do. No, I'm not a minority or a foreign exchange student. I am a white man born in America. And yet, I do not understand 15% of what people say.

Why is that? Because it's designed that way! If we all spoke the language it took to make it in life there would be no McDonalds employees. Our favorite Meal Deal would not have a way to the plate.

We all have a multitude of options at our fingertips, and not to hurt your feelings, but we all are to stupid to recognize it. Even me, for a very long time. In the age of computers, we are dinosaurs.

Here is the key, "you can Google anything." You want to make money online. Google can help you. Believe me.

Google 'Making Money from Home' and you will end up buried in Search criteria. Trust me. And they will show you ad after ad, and video after video.

I know because I did it. Everything from Amazon to Zip Recruiter, and I do mean everything.

Affiliate Marketing, Niche Marketing, Drop Shipping, Fabrication. Everything. It comes down to this, even those things leave you with table scraps. Some larger than others. So how do you "make it", you ask? With guidance from me. Because let's face it, money makes the world go 'round.

For me a Solid Foundation was a business doing what I know and what I love. I'm a Tattoo Artist. I own Infamous Ink & Custom Paints. We do tattoos, we airbrush cars. It still left me a slave. Working back-breaking hours to stay ahead.

See, here in lies the problem. We must sleep. So, all that down time kills the pocket. I'm a workaholic because I had to be. My study of making money online only cost me money because I couldn't understand what I was reading. Until recently.

See, I made everything too complicated, not because it was complicated but because I was trying to pinpoint that key element that these guys had.

I completely missed the whole concept. Keep reading for this is the process I used to make it online. I built an empire that is still growing, and I will show you how too. Whether it's a business start-up or strictly online education you need. It's all right here.

THE HYPE

We all want a job that's not a job. I know I would love to change the word "<u>work</u>" in the dictionary to "fun". No matter how enticing this notion is, it is unrealistic at best.

As I said, Google can provide you with a plethora of ideals to whet your appetite. Using words like "Even you can…" or pushbutton commission, "It's as easy as 1,2,3…" I know you've seen at least one banner ad claiming to have the secret to wealth online.

"Sign up today and we will do the rest!" For a minimum deposit. Or terms like, "$2.99 we will set up your cash commission system". Yeah, we've all heard them. We've all laughed, and silently wondered, if maybe there truly is something to be learned. There is Ladies and Gentlemen! But you have to read between the lines, otherwise you will miss it completely. Because, let's face it, you were taught to

"Supersize" your dumbass instead of how to create financial freedom. Please, it's not your fault entirely.

The Elite would deny the knowledge I am going to reveal in this book simply because they are rich and lazy. If we all knew how to make money like them, who would make them money so they can continue to be lazy. Never worrying about their bills because "we" make sure their bills are paid while ours go delinquent.

This book is full of resources to open, operate, fund, and expand businesses. If being your own boss appeals to you, please continue reading this book.

I will shed light on the "complexities of owning a business." I need you all to know, I actually laughed writing that sentence. There are a lot of counterparts needed to open and run a viable business.

Licenses
Permits
Bookkeeping
Payroll
Accounting

Social Networking
Marketing
Advertising
eCommerce
Inventory

Who knows the amount of red tape your chosen field may require? What if I told you all you need to know to make it in life is four words? Literally, four.
All you need to know…are you ready?
        OUT GURU THE GURUS!!

All these commercials about getting a degree, PhDs, Bachelors, yada-yada. It's all an illusion. From our childhood, we are hyped, brainwashed by our parents and grandparents to go to school, get a good job with a retirement package. Pay our taxes to better our society, fix our roads, broaden our horizons. It's all one giant farce. We have been duped. Ask yourselves, "Are your neighborhood roads nice?"

Has your taxes paid for Crime Watch on your block? Have they kept thieves, speeders or crooked cops from wreaking havoc on the public? Nope! Nope!! And Nope!!!

That's because your tax dollars don't go to schools or nonprofit organizations. Your tax dollars go to your State Senator's Bentley, Mercedes or Lexus.

We pay for their way of life in the pursuit of laziness. Put simply, it's easier to sit and let you make me a fortune than go work for it myself. I am down with OPP, that is, Other People's Profits. Sad but true.

I promise you this, I will not take your money and not give you what I told you I would. I will stay with you as long as it takes to get you where you want to go.

For one on one coaching go to
contact@infamous-ink.com

More than anything in this life, my word means everything to me. This is not a get rich quick scheme. Nor is it a no risk package with a fancy button

I own Infamous Ink & Custom Paints and Infamous Ink Publishing. I am an award-winning artist. A published author of many Books:
- An Illustrated Book of Realism Tattoos
- Infamous Tattoo Coloring Book #1
- Infamous Tattoo Coloring Book #2
- From the Cage to the Stage: An Ex-Con's Guide to Financial Stability
- Bunny Hops Home
- Bunny Hops ABCs
- Sam & Bandit Save the Day
- Blood Rose

And many more.

The kick in the pants, I didn't go to school, college or vocational education! I have a GED. I dropped out when I was in 9th grade.

So, if telling yourself you can't is good enough, close this book and pass it along to someone who may benefit from a little boost to their everyday lives.

Put your big boy pants on and get ready to change your life. What stories do you want to tell your children?

I can show you how! I can lead you down the path, the decision is yours though.

For Consulting:
contact@infamous-ink.com
or call Kathy (509) 560-5155

It's your time to shine. Pick a location and together we can get you there.

SMOKE & MIRRORS

Just recently, I decided to be a publisher. For a greedy reason, I admit. I want all of my money. Yes, I am one of those guys. Haha. Let's face it, so are you, or you wouldn't be reading my book.

Anyhow, I had a very good friend of mine, who just happens to be a business associate of mine, look into what it takes to open a publishing company. The packet of printouts were quite daunting, I must say, a hundred pages or so. I began to read.

This packet is full of information, all of it equally sufficient in its own right. The steps were there. Each a push in the right direction. As I read, I began to notice that all "direction" the writer was giving was extremely vague. For instance, and I quote, "You must get a business license" and "Pick an entity".

Do any of you know what that means? I love Amazon, kdp.com is an awesome platform to begin on. However, they leave an agonizing gap of misinformation for those of us who do not know how to code a computer. Let's face it, we do not speak "the language".

    Further I read, and further I began to see what was happening. The information being given to help "us" … is cloaked in website links buried in someone's personal code. Most likely a pay-per-click site that allows people to learn by visiting a website that will do it for you for a subscription price.

    I'm not knocking their system. I too believe it's a very well thought out gig. However, I have something they do not. Dignity and Honor. I could never tell you I will show you how to achieve your dreams and leave you hanging on a branch in the wind.

    As I kept reading, I became a little perturbed because I was falling down the rabbit hole. The closer I got to a reveal, poof, we turned a corner and it was just gone, immersed in a quagmire of nothing.

    The Hype was there. Keep the reader excited, hooked with a promise to deliver, to produce. Only to be left with nothing. I wasted two hours reading, looking. Totally dumbfounded. I truly thought I missed it. So, I started to read it again.

    People, if you read something looking for answers, it costs time you will never get back.

And if you don't find any answers it's not because you're stupid. It's simply the design.

If I told you I have the answer, and I give it to you, or sell it to you, then my worth becomes your worth. Doesn't seem so smart, does it? Supply and Demand.

If I told you I have the answer, would you believe me? I'm going to show you how it's done. Below you'll read an inflamed informational promising the key to making wealth online.

DISCLAIMER: ANY SIMILARITIES THIS EXAMPLE HAS TO ANY WEBSITE OR EDUCATIONAL ENTITY IS COMPLETELY BY CHANCE.

EXAMPLE:

"Starting your own online business is an important step to making money online. Whether you are selling your own merchandise or someone else's. Or if you just want to protect yourself and your assets.

For many starting a business is a tedious, time consuming feat, and stress is downright painful.

Don't worry, this Step by Step Guide coupled with some seriously dazzling online services, we can help you determine if you are ready to start a business.

_____

Do you see what is happening here? You have been separated, so uneducated that YOU, yes you, even believe you cannot do this without the writer's help.

First, they scare you with words like "tedious" and "downright painful", or my personal favorite "protect yourself". These terms do not spark confidence in the reader. They are not supposed to.

The writer's goal is to convince you that you are not strong, or smart enough, without their super-secret squirrel shit.

Yes, I said shit. I do not believe in pulling punches.

Back to example:
"I have enlisted help from Katherine Elizabeth from (onlinemillionaire.com) to provide some updates, and feedback on this article. A lot has changed since I set up my Business, and Kathy brings the experience of helping thousands of individuals, just like you, set up systems to manage operations.

In This Article You Will Learn:

1. Pro's and con's of Business management
2. When is the proper time for you to start your business
3. How to start your online business
4. Options for setting up safely

Before I dive too deep, I must make two Disclaimers:

1. At this time, I am no lawyer, though I have set up my business. It is best to seek legal advice before taking action.
2. If you follow the steps to my article, I am in no way claiming or guaranteeing you will make money.

So here, do you see what just happened?!

1. They enlisted the "help" of an "expert" whom I guarantee works at their website.
2. They listed all this propaganda on pro's and con's to doing the set up.
3. And finally, they alleviate all responsibility of their claim to make you money by a Disclaimer saying they are in no way saying they will make you money.

In this book, I will give you legitimate references to help your Journey to Stability.
And with that said, let's begin.

EXAMPLE:

Before we jump into the process of setting up your online business, let's first look to see why you should do it.

- *Having a business conveys Professionalism*
- *Gives you certain protections with work and assets*
- *Allows you to manage your own Intellectual Property*
- *Continuity of business*
- *Maintain control over your work*
- *Shifts mindset from Hobby to business owner*
- *Fulfills your dream of being the boss*

See, there are many benefits to starting your own online business.
Read further for more clarity on benefits, or if you are already clear, skip next chapter.

This section is clearly a Blast Freezer to illicit negative thoughts to slowly creep into your mind.

The term "Basically" means the minimal amount of knowledge, of any one thing, and the writer crushes your self-confidence with the words.

"If you are already clear, skip to next chapter." Knowing you still have not been given the Golden Goose yet. Because "Basically" the writer believes you to be too stupid to do it without them. Otherwise, his/her website would not be the only links to the informational.

Having sufficiently cooled your enthusiasm, now they have to hook you again.

EXAMPLE:

PROTECT YOURSELF

Although it's rare, lawsuits can happen! It happened to me. I was sued for a false claim.

If you don't have a business, and you get sued, then your personal reputation, finances and Public Record will be at risk.

Starting a business gives you legal protection and helps distinguish between the business's finances and your personal finances. The courts, or collection agencies could only come after your company's assets.

Sound advice, but seriously lacking in direction. All entities are different in what they "can and cannot do" for your business. For instance, a sole proprietor still leaves your personal finances at risk. It's extremely selective. The Elite do not want to lose their place on the Corporate ladder.

EXAMPLE:

Subscribe on iTunes
https://onlinemillionaire.com/startup/itunes
Listen on Google Play
https://onlinemillionaire.com/googleplay
Subscribe Stitcher
https://onnlinemillionaire.com/stitcher

I got sued...so I started an LLC...it used to be a pain...but now it's easy as 1-2-3 #onlinemillionaire
Click to Tweet
https://twitter.com/share

It's as easy as 1-2-3+%onlinemillionaire URL= (https://onlinemillionaire.com/makemoneyonline)

_____

    All these links belong to the writer of this propaganda. They are real in every way. They will link you to someone, or somewhere, with more info.

    However, to do so will cost you. Don't believe me, go click and see for yourself. Guess what? You still don't know how to do anything. This informational has only asked you what you would like to do and given you links to click on which require a subscription to visit. A low monthly fee, but a fee, nonetheless.

    I don't know about you, but I want something if I have to pay something. Quid! Pro! Quo!

Though, not all is a loss. There are things to be learned from these informationals. For instance, you now see how they hook you in. They have to keep you believing it is so complicated that no matter how badly you want to be one of the Elite, you will never engage simply because they want you to pay them to do exactly what they have been doing from the start.

I'm here to shed light on this "secret". Revealing things of this nature could cost me money in the long run, for I could do like the rest of the Elite, but that is not honorable. If you can read, you can make money. The key is reading between the lines. What is this example telling you?

___

EXAMPLE:

A company is a unique entity, in that like a person it can enter into contracts, sue people and other entities. It can also be sued. It can own assets free of it its owner. A company is afforded the same rights as that of a person. This allows you Peace of Mind that your company will keep growing and be safe, while leaving you safe.

Assuring continuity of your company is as easy as having a well written operating system. The operating agreement dictates how your company conducts its affairs. A properly organized LLC can continue in perpetuity.

This means properly allocated shares, stocks, platforms, etc., can be managed after or if you become incapacitated or deceased.

Now this section above was full of good, sound advice. Facts you can check to solidify your decision, however, it still has not given you any guidance on doing or starting on your own. It silently hints that the reader is still uneducated enough to do this without the writer's help.

In the chapters to come, I will show you some more examples, but I will also show you what you, "let's face it" probably are still missing.

The whole point of these informational "Do It Yourself" platforms are built to push you into letting someone else do it for you. Offering good, logical advice, yet leading you into self-doubt.

I guarantee you, not one writer of these "Golden Key" Gurus will appreciate what I'm doing here. Do you care? I don't. This is the land of the free, isn't it?

If it is, then why are we all living in fear? Why do we all let these people beat us down and make us think we are not worthy of the "American Dream"? This is America, isn't it?

What will your future be?

FACT FINDER!

1. Starting a business opens the door to tax write offs.
2. Allows you to work for clients and customers, not employers.
3. Allows you to name the pay rate for your services.
4. Gives you power to decide the direction of your business.
5. Leaves you something to give to family when you are gone.

Why do we work? Is it for money? Ask yourself this, and if you actually think about this question you will see "it is" and "isn't" correct.

Yes, it's for money. However, it's really for the freedom that money provides.

Time is what we work for.

Time for children, family or even significant others. The "Golden Rule" that we were taught was flawed. Creating slaves instead of individuals with hopes and dreams of our own. You all deserve the truth.

It's time to climb the ladder, for your families. I challenge you to step out of your 9-5 and put on an honest attempt at happiness. It's not a myth. You won't search forever for a unicorn, I promise. I am an uneducated man with a GED. Won't you at least try?

I'm available for consulting. My business associate is available for consulting.

contact@infamous-ink.com
info@infamous-ink.com

The only thing stopping you is you. Keep reading for a glimpse at getting started with a start-up. I will lead you step by step to owning a business of your own. Getting started is just one step of becoming free financially.

HARSH REALITY

    We live, each and everyone of us, in a time where the majority of the population believe that they are owed something. This "entitlement epidemic" is so thick that it is destroying the fabric of society, breeding weak minded, unmotivated children.
    Why should they want to work? They truly believe that we, the last of the working class, owe them, simply because they exist.
    I'm betting you won't have to think too long before you reach a name of an individual you know who is one of such examples. I know more than 50, sadly. Some of them I actually care for, which makes it 3 times as hard to turn my back on them.
    And, I'm pretty sure at least a few of you know what I'm talking about. The woman who touched my heart, and gave me a reason to fight for something, the one who made this all possible

for me, and you, chose to give up and quit having a dream. Please, to all of you, Don't Give Up!

If the example we set is to give up, what will our children do? They will do exactly what we did. So, for you, for us, for them, we have to fight the pursuit of laziness.

I'm not preaching to attract followers. I am content standing on my own, alone. I am a man. I have already made my choice. And, I will stand by that choice through whatever end it produces.

Perhaps there is one of you, even one, who can benefit from what I'm doing here. If so, it is worth all the effort I have put into it. And I hope it's worth it to Katherine, my associate, who has also put in the effort.

Together, we have a bond. Both of us are dreaming for ourselves, but more importantly for her, she is living a dream for her son who is a drug addict.

Myself, I'm living a dream for a woman I love so dearly who is a heroin junkie. We share a shadow of pain and anguish that helps fuel our cause. We are fighting for the ones who have given up before they even got started.

Pull the curtain open and see what is really going on next door, down the street, or even in your own living room.

Do not turn a blind eye on this. We are the pavement of the future. If we do not produce the way for our children, we will be lost.

We all need to lead. Lead your children. This Generation have a skewed ideal of what it means to move someone. Believing that everyone wants to hear about all these "things" they have that really, they don't.

They lie to each other. Telling them what they "want" to hear. People pleasing. Or, shock factor. Whatever you choose to call it.

Come on, I'm sure some of you have told someone you would do something for them, and really, honestly had no intention of doing it. It's an extremely bad habit, one I'm sure most of us are guilty of. Yes, most of us.

Or, when asked if you had something they could borrow, you lied instead of telling them the truth. It's easier that way, right?

No! Examples. We lead and teach by example. Tell the truth, no matter how uncomfortable it makes you. People will respect it, and you, more.

BASICS & NECESSITIES

The Basics are just that. The reason starting a business is "So Hard" is because you actually have to do something. Motivation is hard to come by. Trust me.

1. For me, the first step to opening a business was realizing what I enjoy doing. Not what I knew how to do, but actually enjoy doing. Ask yourself what you love to do.
   This should be where you start your climb up the corporate ladder to Elite Status.
2. "Consider" education requirements for said industry. Note that I did not say run out and enroll in school. Again, I have a GED.
3. If you do not know the necessary scholastic requirements, don't fret. Find someone you know who does and hire them (i.e.) If you don't know anyone, Zip Recruiters, Angie's

List, Linkdin and several other places have multitudes of candidates.
4. Make the leap. Choose a business structure and get started.

BUSINESS STRUCTURES

SOLE PROPRIETOR:
    This structure is a common, simple type of business ownership. If you are in business by yourself and obtain a business license, you are a sole proprietor.
    It is appropriate for small businesses. Federal income taxes flow through the individual and are reported on the business owner's schedule C. However, a sole proprietorship offers no protection from individual liability, thus leaving owner responsible for lawsuits, and insurance coverage.

PARTNERSHIP:
    Is similar to a sole proprietorship. If you are in business with at least one other person. The partnership is viable even if they have not formalized a partnership agreement.
    A partnership agreement sets forth the rights and obligations of each party and describes what would happen to their interest in the business should one of them die or wish to sell their portion of the business.
    A partnership tax return is required for this structure. However, each partner pays their share

instead of the business paying the taxes and offers no protection to the individual owners.

CORPORATION:

A corporation is formed by filing articles of incorporation through the Secretary of State office. One, or more, individuals can create a corporation. A key initial decision in opening a corporation is whether it should be a C-Corporation or an S-Corporation.

A C-Corp pays taxes on a federal level, corporate and shareholders. A S-Corp only pays taxes on a shareholder level. Certain qualifications must be met to register as an S-Corporation. A corporate structure offers individual protection from lawsuits and insurance. A legal adviser is often advisable in this structure for tax codes change often.

LLC:

A limited liability company, or LLC, is formed by filing a Certificate of Formation with the Secretary of State's office. One, or more individuals can create an LLC.

An LLC may be taxed in different ways. Consult with your accountant in order to make and informed decision about how your LLC will be taxed and file the corresponding documents with the IRS.

Similar to a corporation, a properly formed and maintained LLC can offer protections against individual liability.

Having established the different structures, there are 2 key factors in deciding which structure you should choose.

1. What type of potential liabilities does your chosen field of business face? And, can you purchase adequate insurance for these potential threats?
2. What tax savings/incentives would I receive from forming a business "entity"?

ENTITY:
The structure in which you choose to operate your business (i.e. sole proprietor, partnership, etc.)

To beat the odds and ensure your business is successful, you need to be Pro-active and conscious of your business' strengths and weaknesses. Assemble a team to help you cover all bases of operation.

Check with a legal advisor to make sure you have up to date information on taxes, insurance, bonding, etc. You do not want to get started only to get set back by not having current information.

The appendix has many resources. As I am a current resident of Washington state, its references are local. However, you can Google each state's offices, such as The Small Business Association.

Office of the Secretary of State
www.sos.wa.gov/corps

To register a business, you must contact the Secretary of State.

Even if you are choosing to make money online, whether it's web based business, trading platforms, Affiliate Marketing, you need to check with the Secretary of State as well as the State's Department of Revenue to see if any special permits, licenses or registrations are needed for your chosen industry.

Once you have cleared license/registration requirements you must submit a Trade/Business name search to name your company. Trademark infringement and Copyright laws are very real and unforgiving of ignorance.

Trade name search is to provide a record of all owners of a business. The right to use a Tradename belongs to the one who uses it first in connection with their business. A trade name will remain registered indefinitely until the owner requests that it be cancelled.

You can find trade name registration online with the State's business and professional license search at example:

https://bls.dor.wa.gov/licenseSearch
or Google Trade Name Search.

Google offers many options. Keyword searches, for example:

Register My Business will pull up all local business registration offices for most states. You can also add the state of your request to the search criteria.

Or, if you are busy working your 9-5 to pay your bills, you can get a consult for a couple of dollars or pay to have it done for you by a professional. For consults or services:

contact@infamous-ink.com
info@infamous-ink.com
or call Infamous Ink, Inc
509-560-5155

Our associates are eager to help, for only a few ever really take a step to becoming financially free. Our service rates vary depending on time, but I assure you we offer a fair price for our services.

FEDERAL AGENCIES:

Internal Revenue Service (IRS)
www.irs.gov
Tax Questions? 1-800-829-4933
To Order Forms 1-800-829-3676
www.irs.gov/business/small/index.html
Visit the IRS online Learning and Educational link (above), to see a list of Small Business video and audio presentations, as well as other learning tools.

OTHER RELEVANT IRS TOPICS:

BUSINESS STRUCTURES:
When starting a business, you must decide which entity form your business should take. This will decide which tax return you must file.

SELF EMPLOYMENT TAX:
Everyone must pay Social Security and Medicare taxes. If you are self-employed, your Social Security/Medicare contribution is made through the self-employment tax. Payments made quarterly through form 1040ES.

BUSINESSES WITH EMPLOYEES:
All businesses who employ, withhold income taxes, Social Security and Medicare (FICA), as well as pay the employer's portion of Social Security taxes and pay federal unemployment tax under certain circumstances. Nonpayment of federal taxes can result in penalties and audits, also can result in the closing of your business.

EMPLOYER IDENTIFICATION NUMBER (EIN):
Employers, and most types of businesses are required to have an EIN. To apply for an EIN online, go to:

www.irs.gov

IRS BUSINESS & SPECIALTY TAX LINE:
1-800-829-4933
Monday – Friday
7:00am – 10:00pm (pst)

OSHA:
Occupational Safety & Health Administration
www.ohsa.gov
(A division of the U.S. Dept. of Labor that regulates working conditions.)

EMPLOYER WAGE REPORTING SERVICE CENTER:
www.ssa.gov/employer
1-800-772-6270
Help with all your wage filing responsibilities.

SOCIAL SECURITY ADMINISTRATION:
www.ssa.gov
1-800-772-1213
All employees, employers and self-employed individuals are required to participate in the Social Security program. Employers are required to withhold a fixed percentage of employee's wages, match each employee's contribution and make periodic deposits to the IRS. It is the same for self-employed persons.

U.S. CENSUS BUREAU:
www.census.gov
The leading source of quality data about the Nation's people and economy.

U.S. DEPT OF LABOR (DOL)
www.dol.gov
Telephone Information Center
1-866-487-9243
Regulates working conditions, wages and payment practices.

There are many online workshops with good advice and educational videos and audio instructionals.

EXAMPLE:
workshops@sba.gov

When opening a business, Intellectual Property is more often worth more to a business than liquid assets.

Intellectual Property=
Business Strategies
Images
Concepts & Ideals

You must protect Intellectual Property just like you would protect physical assets. To protect Intellectual Property:

FEDERAL COPYRIGHTS:
www.copyright.gov
Public Information Office 202-707-3000
Forms Hotline 202-707-9100

Copyright is a form of protection provided by the laws of the United States.
(Title 17, U.S.Code) To Authors of original works of authorship, including literary, dramatic, musical, artistic and certain other intellectual works.

FEDERAL PATENTS:
U.S. Patent and Trademark Office
www.uspto.gov
703-308-4357 or 1-800-786-9199
Arlington, VA
A Brand name is a Trademark, protected under the laws set forth by the USPTO. Business logos and other specialized business memorabilia are protected as well.
Catch Phrases are trademark worthy
Graphics.
Designs.
Signatures.
All are items which should be Trademark protected.

 Once you search and secure a trade name, register it with the Secretary of State. Having chosen your entity, it's time to start work.

 Location, location, location! Home based businesses, web-based businesses and Affiliate Marketing can be done from your home. Even if you do not have a website.

AFFILIATE MARKETING:
   To do this type of business, a physical location is not necessary. Affiliate Marketing is posting someone's business ads on your web page for a commission of the sales generated from your web page.
   Don't have a site? Not a problem. These types of ads can be placed on Facebook, Twitter, Instagram, etc. Link ads to your favorite social media site for your favorite products.
   All you have to do is CONTACT the producer of products you wish to sell on your social media site, whether by phone or online (i.e. www.worldwidetattoo.com) find the Contact Us button and ask about Affiliate Marketing for their products. They will be happy to help.
   Any product, any site. Affiliate Marketing is only 1 platform to online wealth.
Visa
Kay Jewelers
Ace Cash
Any site provides Affiliate Marketing. Whatever suits your fancy.

CONSULTING:
   If you know something well, and don't wish to do that something, consult people who want to do these things. For Instance:
   My father was a diesel mechanic. I know how to build diesel engines. I don't care to. Yet, I know how to get into schools. I know the certifications needed to qualify for the field.

All I would have to do is get a business license for a home-based business and teach people how to get started on the path to becoming a diesel mechanic.

Or, do exactly what I am doing right here and now. I am consulting and educating both at the same time. For many different reasons, for many different friends, I have told my stories hoping to shed light on the capability in every one of you.

I would imagine at least once in your life you have heard "if you can think it, you can achieve it."
<u>Only you can stop the growth in your life, You can accomplish anything you set your mind to!</u> I know you've heard that. It's become the "norm" to not believe it anymore.

You think it was any less time consuming or frustrating for any one of hundreds of innovators we have had in our lifetime? The answer is no. The difference is They didn't give up. They refused to take "you can't" for an answer.

If I told you, tomorrow we would go to war, would you believe me? Why not? It's a completely plausible theory.

What if I told you, you too, can make a million dollars? Why not? Also, possible.

I'll tell you why, because you've already embraced the people who have told you, "you can't". They tell you, "you can't", and you believe it, without even trying. Simply because it's easier.

What if I told you, your child was gonna pass away if you didn't try? As horrible as the thought is, wouldn't you give every ounce of blood in your body to do it to protect your children?

<u>Why do you see sitting stagnant any different than the above example?</u> Too many children have nothing because their parents have nothing. Their parents quit trying to make a world for their children and embraced the "I can't" attitude.

With this perspective, they never will. It's a completely sad realization. The very reasons we believe "we cannot" are the very reason why we should strive to be better. To be more.

Here in lies the problem. Our schools only teach slavery. They are not prepared to show our children how to become innovators, because our leaders don't want entrepreneurs, they want servants. People programmed to care for their needs, not our own.

When was the last time you heard of a Government Official, flipping burgers or running out of gas? You don't because they are pampered by the money their fathers and grandfathers own.

Their oath doesn't protect freedom or <u>our</u> way of life, because they see themselves as our superiors.

I don't know about you, but I refuse to be a stepping stool, or a crutch to someone who could care less about me or my children.

<u>You've got it hard you say?</u> <u>So much worse than others.</u> I am a convicted felon several times over, and here I am a business owner. Not once, but over and again. I am a man with a dream, and the motivation to do.

<u>I make shit happen</u>. It's time you did too. I'm doing it for Johanna and her daughters, for my family who have given up. For Kathy's family. It's time to get on the people's side of up. Destiny is not just a corner in a nonexistent town. Embrace yours.

<u>PUBLISHING:</u>
My personal favorite. I am a writer. Yes, I've emailed manuscripts to agent after agent to get on the map. Amazon is amazing.

Publishing is one of the easiest things to do now days because you don't need an agent thanks to eBooks.

Publishing is a great form of residual income, bringing money over and over to your pocket. In fact, I publish my own and other people's works. Not just books either. I publish kid's books, Tattoo magazine, Tattoo calendars, artwork, etc. The sky is literally the limit.

I only suggest you find your niche and capitalize on it. And the same start up rules apply to this as any other field of expertise. Trademark and Copyright laws protect you and the works you publish, even if they are for someone else.

All trades up to this point are simple to get started. Follow the instructions I have laid out. Different fees for different licenses but in the grand scheme of things, it's a lot cheaper than letting somebody else get your hard-earned wages.

My disclaimer is entirely different. Following this outline in no way guarantees you will make millions. However, following this outline will produce an environment in which you choose how to spend your time.

Yes, my time is valuable, but I promise to teach you how to start taking control of your life. Some people are completely content to let others run their lives for them. Most in fact. It's a shame that we, as a people quit striving to do better. Join me and leave something behind for your children and their children.

Now, there is a lot in this book. Earmark pages if need be.

NECESSITIES:
1. A desire to be your own boss.
2. Motivation to take control of your life.
3. A phone.
4. An hour a day to set up your business.
5. A marketable product people want.

WEB SITES

If it is 'working from home' that you desire, first you have to decide in what capacity you wish to do so.

Many corporations allow a service called "Drop Shipping". It is extremely easy to do. Contact any company via Google or direct contact on their website.

EXAMPLE 1:

AMAZON MARKETPLACE
Amazon is one of the Nation's leading retail establishments around the world. Amazon will "Give you" a niche in their storefront. They will set you up a webpage, accessible by you to sell Amazon products. All you have to do is fill orders. Based on sales made by your store, provided by them.

Don't have any products? Not to worry, Amazon will provide the products. If you have your own products? Sell them on your store front! You can sell your own and Amazon's as well, if you choose to.

Hell, you can even sell your favorite products via your favorite sites by copy, cutting and pasting your unique URL provided by Amazon or eBay. Both platforms are very similar. Paste your URL in the "Buy Button" and email and all sales generated by your store front can be linked to your bank card.

Both platforms have tutorials on linking your unique link to your debit/bank card. Yes, you can even link a prepaid or a PayPal card. Ladies and Gentlemen, this is perhaps the easiest way to make money online.

Don't have a place to store inventory? No problem. You don't have to. They will store it in their warehouse.

1. Contact the County Clerk and ask for the Zoning Commissioner. Ask the Zoning Commissioner if your residence needs to be zoned for Commercial Business. Chances are, for the above-mentioned type of business, you will not need to be zoned for Commercial Business.
2. Contact County Clerk and ask if there are any special requirements to start this business (i.e. licenses, permits or certificates). Every state has requirements. Most are affordable. For instance, I can get a General Contractors

license for about $37 a year at the Clerk's office. County Clerks are usually located in or near your County Courthouse.

Information is available on Google, or in a phone book for your surrounding area.

Don't fret if Drop Shipping is not for you. I completely understand, it was not for me. If you have a skill you believe people will buy but no way to market it, you probably need a website.

<u>*Now Many Places Offer Free Websites:*</u>

GoDaddy   Wordpress
Wix.com   Web.com

And many more. Simply Google free "website builder" and choose from the results to begin. Most are fairly easy to choose from. They supply templates to get started.

I own sites on 3 of the 4 listed above. They will help build your custom site and give you access to a domain name. With this approach you can own your own ideal.

EXAMPLE 2:

Say you are a landscaper. You have worked for the same company for several years. Whether it is pushing a mower or installing shrubs, sprinklers, or all of the above, and want to do it yourself.

Contact the County Clerk, get a General Contractors license. Design your website to suit your skill set. Post your ads for your business on LinkedIn, Home Advisor, Angie's List, etc.

If landscaping is too physical for you, not to worry.

EXAMPLE 3:

What if you make candies? Design your site to fit your skill. Again, contact Clerk of your County. Check for licenses required, and <u>this example requires a Food Handler's permit.</u> However, it is still simple to set up.

No matter what your interest, you can sell yourself. What if you don't have a skill set, you ask? My answer to you is, Yes, you do! Everyone has something they love to do.

You can post ads to your Facebook for whatever services you can provide. All you Facebookers, you too can make money from your favorite platform.

Download "Shutterstock". It's a free app on Google Play Store. Google will buy your favorite photos you take with your phone. Plus, you can market them on Facebook. Follow the tutorial on the app and start making money from your Smartphone.

The possibilities are endless. Wanna make money by watching movie previews? Google: How to make money watching "You Tube". It's all possible, right now. For more info go to:
www.infamous-ink.com
info@infamous-ink.com
or call for a consultation at 509-560-5155

OPTIONS

- Business Ownership
- Franchising
- Business Management
- Home Based Business
- Web Based Business/Internet Business

All of the above can be formed by contacting the County Clerk's office in the County you reside, or contact the Small Business Administration.

Most businesses require a license to open, though not hard to acquire.

Current resources are in the appendix in this book. If you are not sure what kind of business you wish to do, my colleagues and I consult for a low, reasonable fee.

We offer:
- Financial Advice
- Investment Advice
- Business Plan Builder
- Audio Workshops
- How-To Guides

Do not let the fear of failure cripple you. If owning a business is not for you and you are comfortable working for someone else, we offer employment. However, if you are just unsure of what to do, please contact us.

Our Apprenticeship programs will teach you "How to do what you want and placement in an environment performing the acquired skillset, in a stable environment.

For information on Apprenticeship programs contact Kathy at:
info@infamous-ink.com

Our rates are reasonable, so are our associates. Build a dream for your future!

Four our investment platform contact:
info@infamous-ink.com
or call 509-560-5155

THE FOLLOWING PAGES CONTAIN ADDITIONAL RESOURCES THAT MAY BE HELPFUL TO YOU

APPENDIX RESOURCES

SCORE
www.score.org
 SCORE provides counseling, training, business tips and free templates.
 SCORE volunteers work with any start up or existing small business. Connect with a local SCORE mentor to get free and confidential small business advice.

SEATTLE CHAPTER #55
www.seattle.score.org
2401 Fourth Avenue, Ste#450
Seattle, WA 98121-3419
206-553-7320 or 1-877-732-7267
On-site counseling and workshops
Monday – Friday 9:ooam – 4:oopm
SMALL BUSINESS DEVELOPMENT CENTERS
www.wsbdc.org
Washington State University
534 E. Spokane Falls Blvd.
Spokane, WA 99201-1495
Brett Rogers, State Director
Duane Fladland, Associate State Director
509-358-7765
sbdc@wsu.edu

IDAHO

LEWIS AND CLARK STATE COLLEGE
Lewiston, ID
Barbara Leachman 208-792-2465
baleachman@lcsc.edu
Judy Schumacher 208-792-2465
jsschumacher@lcsc.edu

POST FALLS
Workforce Training Center
William Jhung 208-665-6085
William.jhung@nic.edu

SANDPOINT
Bonner Business Center
208-263-4073
isbdc@nic.edu

Every state has these offices. Simply Google any of the above acronyms to find locations in your county and state.

SMALL BUSINESS LOAN GUARANTEE PROGRAM
www.sba.gov/financialassistance
The SBA helps small businesses obtain credit by giving the Government's guarantee to loans made by commercial lenders. Most banks and some credit unions participate in this program.
Find the SBA Participating Lender list at www.sba.gov/wa under resources.

The SBA offers:
Primary Lending Program guarantees are up to $3,750,000 of each loan made by participant lenders. These loans usually range from $25,000 to $5M and are repaid in monthly installments.

The SBA offers streamlined loan processing with:
The Preferred Lender Program
The Express Lender Program
Patriot Express Loans
Export Express Loans

And let's face it, if a loan is not where you wish to start, then the SBA also offers fast track to Small Business Startup/Expansion Grants. Most grants are government funds which you do not have to pay back.

Loans, micro-loans, all capital options are a must study when opening a business. Take time to study the options available, and if you don't have time,

Contact: contact@infamous-ink.com for assistance at infamous-ink.com, we believe in a reasonable price for quality services.

Together, we can find the path that is right for you.

GRANTS

Catalog of Federal Domestic Assistance (CFDA) – www.cfda.gov

Federal Grant Resources
www.grants.gov
A listing of grants available through a variety of federal, state and local organizations.

FirstGov for Nonprofits
www.USA.gov/Business/nonprofit
Grants and other assistance for nonprofits.

The Foundation Center
www.foundationcenter.gov
Private funding sources, how to write a grant proposal, and State libraries with Grant reference collections.

The Grantsmanship Centers Grant
www.tgci.com/funding
Resources by state
State- specific info on community foundations and corporate giving programs.

VENTURE CAPITAL

Small Business Investment Company (SBIC)
Privately owned and managed investment funds. Licensed and regulated by the Small Business Assoc. they use their own capital – plus funds borrowed with an SBAs guarantee.

Bancshares Capital, L.P.
bancshares_lp@msn.com
206-948-1195
Investment Policy Early-Stages high tech. Investment Type: eCommerce, software, digital media, Telecom and healthcare.

Fluke Venture Partners
www.flukeventures.com
425-453-4590
Gabelein@flukeventures.com

NW Entrepreneur Network
www.nwen.org
206-420-0226
info@nwen.org
Helps entrepreneurs build their Network. Provides mentoring and access to investors.

FOR UP-DATES SEE WEBSITE

Infamous Ink, Inc
509-560-5155
Email: contact@infamous-ink.com

www.infamous-ink.com
info@infamous-ink.com

Take the First Step to Your Financial Future!

AMERICAN ARTISTS INCORPORATED

CHECK OUT OTHER WORKS BY JUSTIN AUTREY:
- BLOOD ROSE
- FROM THE CAGE TO THE STAGE: AN EX-CON'S GUIDE TO FINANCIAL STABILITY
- TATTOO COLORING BOOK #1
- TATTOO COLORING BOOK #2

There are several future books coming out to print soon!!

THIS PAGE INTENTIONALLY LEFT BLANK

www.ingramcontent.com/pod-product-compliance
Lightning Source LLC
Chambersburg PA
CBHW040237220526
45473CB00001B/271